The Adventures of Scuba Jack
Copyright 2021 by Beth Costanzo
All rights reserved

While there are plenty of animals on our planet to keep us busy, it's always fun to look back at some of Earth's prehistoric animals. These prehistoric animals aren't with us anymore, but their size, behavior, and even ferocity are simply fascinating.

Today, I want to talk about one of those prehistoric animals. That animal is the **woolly mammoth**. The woolly mammoth was a huge animal that roamed our planet thousands of years ago. But even though they aren't walking Earth, scientists have recently been able to extract blood from an ancient woolly mammoth. This little amount of blood may help scientists and researchers learn so much more about this gigantic prehistoric creature.

The woolly mammoth lived during the last ice age. They lived from about five million years ago to about 4,000 years ago. During its existence on Earth, the woolly mammoth was found on continents like Africa, Asia, Europe, and North America. Even though most of the woolly mammoth population died out around 10,000 years ago, it is believed that a population of around 500 to 1,000 woolly mammoths lived on an island in the Arctic Ocean until 1650 BC.

Whenever you think of the woolly mammoth, you likely picture a huge, towering creature with a lot of fur. While woolly mammoths were big, they weren't tens or hundreds of feet tall. Instead, male woolly mammoths were around 9 to 11 feet tall and weighed about 13,000 pounds. Female woolly mammoths, on the other hand, were about 8.5 to 9.5 feet tall and weighed around 8,000 pounds.

If you were to compare the woolly mammoth to a modern-day animal, the closest comparison would be the elephant. Compared to the modern-day elephant, however, the woolly mammoth's ears are shorter. The woolly mammoth needed these shorter ears because they would protect them from heat loss and frostbite.

Beyond its height and weight, one of the woolly mammoth's most famous features is its fur. The woolly mammoth needed this fur because it lived during the last ice age. Even though we think of the woolly mammoth having orange-colored fur due to the famous movie Ice Age, woolly mammoths had fur in both light and dark colors. Along with this distinctive fur, woolly mammoths had long and curved tusks. These tucks were about 15 feet long. Woolly mammoths would use their tusks for things like fighting, foraging, and moving around objects.

As far as their diet, you may think that woolly mammoths were fierce creatures who liked to hunt other animals. It turns out that these animals were herbivores, meaning that they did not eat meat. Woolly mammoths liked to eat grass, but they would also eat things like plants and flowers.

Caveman art showing a Woolly Mammoth

Even though woolly mammoths don't exist today, some of our earliest ancestors lived among them. It is thought that around 30,000 to 40,000 years ago, humans lived with woolly mammoths in Africa. Humans would hunt these animals for food. They would also use the bones and tusks from woolly mammoths to make things like art, dwellings, and tools.

Woolly mammoths made quite an impression on our early ancestors. Our ice age ancestors were so impressed that they used to make cave drawings of these furry creatures. In France's famous Rouffignac cave, for example, these early humans made 158 depictions of woolly mammoths.

The woolly mammoth was a fascinating creature. Because it roamed the Earth so many years ago, we are still learning about this animal. Scientists and researchers around the world are hard at work, trying to get a better understanding of the woolly mammoth's biological makeup and activity.

One of the more exciting discoveries, however, occurred in 2013. In that year, researchers found a frozen woolly mammoth with a pool of liquid blood in Siberia. This woolly mammoth's name is Buttercup and she died when she was in her 50s. Researchers said that Buttercup's trunk was the most-preserved woolly mammoth trunk that has been found in history. Along with its trunk, the research team found three legs, a majority of Buttercup's body, and part of her head. Even though Buttercup lived thousands of years ago, her body parts were still well-preserved due to the cold in Siberia.

Buttercup the Woolly Mammoth

Those same researchers have been hard at work to learn more about Buttercup. Beyond that, however, the discovered blood presents some interesting possibilities. By extracting this blood, scientists theorized that they could make a clone of Buttercup. This would mean that woolly mammoths could possibly walk our planet again—almost like Jurassic Park!

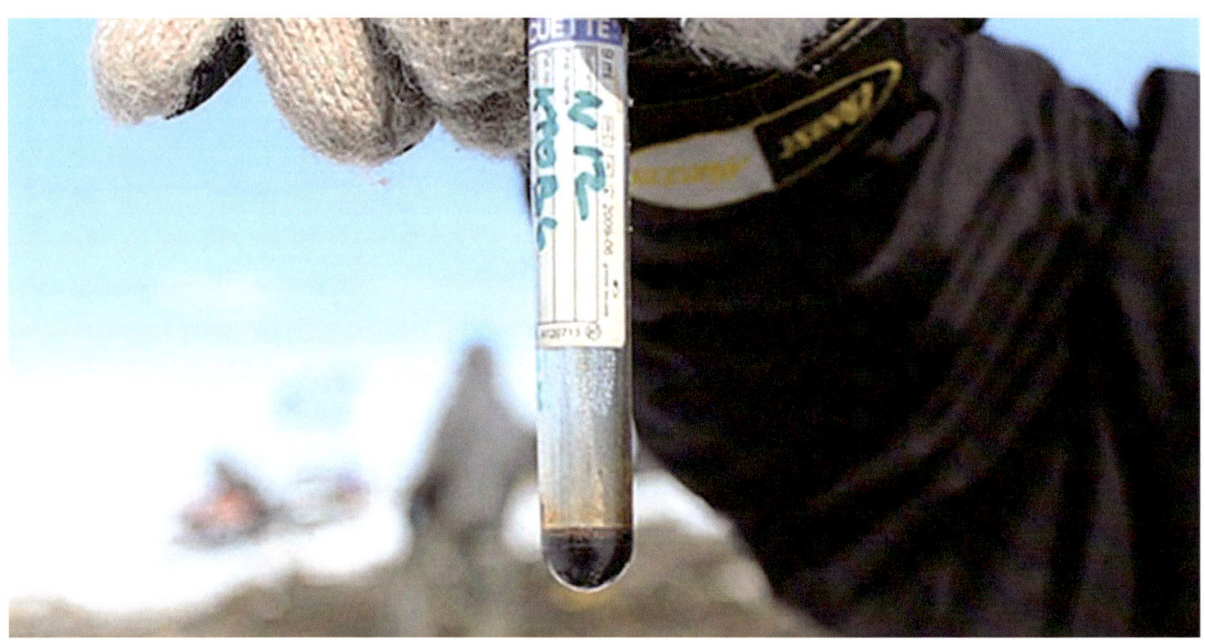

As you know, we still aren't living in a world where woolly mammoths are walking the Earth. Nevertheless, these scientists are still hard at work. In 2015, engineers and geneticists at Harvard University have been working to create a mammoth-elephant hybrid. Basically, these engineers and geneticists are trying to combine the genes of both the woolly mammoth and an Asian elephant. The Asian elephant is the woolly mammoth's closest living relative. There are also scientists in South Korea who are working on this task. These scientists have some similar experience, as they were able to clone dogs several years ago.

There is a worldwide effort to clone the woolly mammoth. While that end goal of a living and breathing woolly mammoth doesn't yet exist, scientists are still trying. When they are successful, it is going to be quite exciting!

The Return of the Woolly Mammoth?

We can't say for sure when the woolly mammoth is going to return. It may be a long time. Whenever it does, however, I hope that you have a great appreciation for this creature. Woolly mammoths walked our planet for thousands of years. Our earliest ancestors were even able to catch a glimpse and use the woolly mammoth to make their lives easier. In the end, the woolly mammoth is one of the most fascinating prehistoric animals. I hope you find them as interesting as I do!

Mammoth mummy

WOOLLY MAMMOTH ACTIVITES

TRACING

Trace the sentence then rewrite it

Woolly Mammoth

COUNTING

Count the mammoths then circle the correct answer

4 6 5    3 4 5

6 5 7    6 7 8

www.adventuresofscubajack.com

MAZE

Help the woolly mammoth to find the exist

www.adventuresofscubajack.com

WORD SEARCH
Find the words listed below

```
D L B R M W L P J Y
E L E P H A N T L Y
H A N Y D N K L D B
T N L A M D O A I D
O C T X M O W G G J
M I N Y W E C I Z E
M E G Q G R V W K Q
A N N N J K Z A P N
M T J M Y X B X C R
```

Woolly
Mammoth
Ancient
Elephant

Caveman
Big
Ice
Age

www.adventuresofscubajack.com

COLORING

Color the image below

www.adventuresofscubajack.com

WOOLLY MAMMOTH CRAFT

You will need:

Scissors
Glue
Coloring Pencils

Directions:

1- Glue the Head to the Body
2- Glue the horns to the head
3- Glue the tail to the back of the body
4- Color your cute Woolly Mammoth!

www.adventuresofscubajack.com

Visit us at:

www.adventuresofscubajack.com

www.ingramcontent.com/pod-product-compliance
Lightning Source LLC
Chambersburg PA
CBRC090837010526
44118CB00007B/239